Whales and Dolphins
AN IMAGINATION LIBRARY SERIES

BOTTLENOSE DOLPHINS

by Victor Gentle and Janet Perry

Gareth Stevens Publishing
A WORLD ALMANAC EDUCATION GROUP COMPANY

Please visit our web site at: **www.garethstevens.com**
For a free color catalog describing Gareth Stevens' list of high-quality books and
multimedia programs, call 1-800-542-2595 (USA) or 1-800-461-9120 (Canada).
Gareth Stevens Publishing's Fax: (414) 332-3567.

Library of Congress Cataloging-in-Publication Data

Gentle, Victor.
    Bottlenose dolphins / by Victor Gentle and Janet Perry.
       p. cm. — (Whales and dolphins: an imagination library series)
    Includes bibliographical references and index.
    ISBN 0-8368-2881-X (lib. bdg.)
    1. Bottlenose dolphin—Juvenile literature. [1. Bottlenose dolphin.
2. Dolphins.] I. Perry, Janet, 1960- II. Title.
QL737.C432G459   2001
599.53'3—dc21   2001020012

First published in 2001 by
Gareth Stevens Publishing
A World Almanac Education Group Company
330 West Olive Street, Suite 100
Milwaukee, WI 53212 USA

Text: Victor Gentle and Janet Perry
Art direction: Karen Knutson
Page layout: Victor Gentle, Janet Perry, Joel Bucaro, and Tammy Gruenewald
Cover design: Joel Bucaro
Series editor: Catherine Gardner
Picture Researcher: Diane Laska-Swanke

Photo credits: Cover © Hiroto Kawaguchi/Seapics.com; p. 5 Photofest; pp. 7, 11,
17, 19 © Doug Perrine/Seapics.com; p. 9 © Dan Burton/Seapics.com; p. 13
© Hiroya Minakuchi/Seapics.com; p. 15 © Jeffrey L. Rotman/CORBIS; p. 21
© James D. Watt/Seapics.com; p. 22 Joel Bucaro/© Gareth Stevens, Inc., 2001

Printed in the United States of America

1 2 3 4 5 6 7 8 9 05 04 03 02 01

Front cover: Bottlenose dolphins are so cute! And yet, our
names for them are not very kind. Even their scientific name,
Tursiops truncatus, means "dolphin with a cut-off nose."

TABLE OF CONTENTS

Words that appear in the glossary are printed in **boldface** type the first time they occur in the text.

THEY CALL HIM "FLIPPER"!

Everyone loved Flipper, the star of a famous 1960s American television series.

He rescued his friends from danger. He learned new tricks instantly. He played catch, he jumped through hoops, he pulled boats, and he made his friends laugh when he played jokes on them. He knew when they were sad and cheered them up. Every kid wanted Flipper for a friend.

In real life, many dolphins played the role of Flipper. Each one had its own personality. Together, they all made us think that, *maybe*, bottlenose dolphins were just as smart as human beings — yet, we hardly knew them!

Female dolphins played Flipper on television. Young females have no battle scars and are easier to capture. Here, one of the Flippers is tailwalking.

NO ONE IS SMARTER THAN HE

It is not easy to study bottlenose dolphins, even though they are fun to watch. We barely understand their underwater world — to us, it is **alien**. Yet, with special equipment and careful study, scientists and trainers have discovered some amazing facts about bottlenose dolphins.

Bottlenoses have learned to live almost anywhere in the ocean. They teach each other to survive. They have complicated relationships with their families and their companions. They seem to use a musical language all their own.

Here, three bottlenoses act on a hand signal from a human. But are we smart enough to learn what dolphins may try to tell us?

DOLPHINS IN THE COLD

Bottlenose dolphins live in all the oceans, near the coasts, and in the deepest seas. Their bodies have slightly different shapes, colors, and sizes that are **adapted** to the many places they live. They also adapt their **behavior** to the places they live.

Bottlenose dolphins living in cold, deep, murky water near Scotland are different from those in warm, clear, shallow seas near northern Australia.

Scottish bottlenoses are dark gray. Their skin blends with the color of the waters where they swim. They swim fast, eat big fish, and have lots of fat to keep them warm in the cold North Sea. Bottlenose dolphins living in warm Australian seas, however, are built to keep from overheating.

This bottlenose dolphin, which lives in the Red Sea, is playing with an octopus. Do you think the dolphin's spotted skin is an **adaptation**?

DOLPHINS IN THE HEAT

Australian bottlenoses are adapted to their warm home, just as Scottish ones are adapted to their cold home. Australian bottlenoses are light gray and blend into the paler, shallower waters near shore.

Larger flippers help Australian bottlenoses lose heat. Less fat helps them keep cool, too. Australian bottlenoses feed on small fish that are easy to catch. By chasing easy **prey**, they can swim more slowly and keep from getting too hot.

Bottlenose dolphins also learn special tricks for catching food, depending on where they live. For example, bottlenoses living in a group off the coast of South Carolina know different fishing tricks than a lone bottlenose living off the coast of Ireland.

JoJo, a lone dolphin in the Caribbean Sea, has many non-dolphin friends. Here, he swims with his pal, Toffee.

ROUND 'EM UP! CHOW TIME!

Bottlenose dolphins that live near the salt marshes of North Carolina wait each day for the tides to drop. Then, they swim fast, herding large groups of fish onto the muddy banks, where the dolphins beach themselves, too! The dolphins grab the flopping fish, then wriggle back into the water.

A lone dolphin living off the western coast of Ireland uses different tricks. It cannot herd fish by itself. So it chases down its meals one by one — maybe a fish first, a squid next, and then a lobster.

Are bottlenoses born knowing exactly how to hunt in their **habitats**? No! They have to learn much of what they do, starting from the day they are born.

Two bottlenoses work together to snatch fish off a mud bank. Their teeth are shaped like the tips of sharpened sticks, perfect for holding prey until it is gulped.

JUST WHISTLE!

Bottlenose mothers carefully teach their **calves** important lessons in hunting, hiding, behaving in company — even breathing!

The first thing a **calf** learns is its mother's "name," or **signature whistle**. A mother whistles to her newborn and swims to the surface with it, to breathe. The calf tries to whistle back to her. During the first days of the calf's life, they whistle to each other, over and over, to get it right. Bottlenose dolphins know each other by their signature whistles.

Scientists believe that bottlenose dolphins **communicate** lessons to each other by showing, by touching, and by "talking" in a unique language of whistles, clicks, moans, caws, and raspberries.

Mother and calf keep close contact as they swim, leap, and breathe. This bond lasts their whole lives, even if they are separated for years at a time.

CALL AND RESPONSE

Bottlenoses touch, "talk," and mate just to stay connected, too. They usually live in groups of 2 to more than 200, with members leaving and joining all the time. Much snuggling and playing keeps everyone happy in all this confusion.

There are frequent battles — for mates, for food, and to protect the group from enemies, such as sharks, **orcas**, other dolphins, and people. So, good communication also keeps everyone out of danger.

Bottlenoses do not use their faces to communicate their feelings. The "smile" we think we see is really just the way their **melons** shape their heads. The melon makes and receives signals that tell them about their world. This process is called **echolocation**.

Their echolocation is so sensitive that bottlenoses can find an object and return it — like this one is doing — even when their eyes are covered.

FRIEND OR FOE?

Just as there are friendly people and mean people, there are friendly and mean bottlenose dolphins. And you never can tell! Bottlenoses behave in ways that are just as confusing as the ways people behave!

Bottlenose males have been seen trying to drown calves to kidnap females. A dolphin may ram a person for petting it the wrong way or for getting between a mother and a calf, or a male and a female.

Bottlenoses are gentle, too. A mother may carry her dead calf on her back for days, grieving, while other dolphins defend her from sharks. Susie, one of the Flippers, flicked a drowning boy onto a dock with her tail and saved his life!

The two bottlenose dolphins at the front of this pack are being chased out of town by a mob of spotted dolphins!

OUR FAVORITE ALIENS

Bottlenose dolphins are a lot like us. They love to show off, play, sing, and touch. They fight, protect, kill, teach, and learn. They are wild, tame, loving, cruel, and beautiful.

Scientists are pretty sure bottlenose dolphins are at least as smart as we are. They know more about the sea than any human. Wouldn't it be great to have a dolphin teacher?

Actor Robin Williams liked dolphins, so he hosted a video studying them. In the video, he says, "If we're really interested in learning to make contact with alien intelligence, maybe we don't have to look to the edge of the galaxy to find them. They're right here, waiting for us."

Bottlenoses blow air out before they breathe in. This one may be blowing bubbles for fun or at the camera! We'll never know if we don't learn their language.

MORE TO READ AND VIEW

Books (Nonfiction)   *Follow That Fin! Studying Dolphin Behavior. Turnstone Ocean Pilot Book*
    (series). Amy Samuels (Raintree Steck-Vaughn)
How Did We Find Out About Life in the Sea? Isaac Asimov (Walker)
Whales and Dolphins (series). Victor Gentle and Janet Perry
    (Gareth Stevens)
Whales, Dolphins, and Porpoises. Mark Carwardine (Dorling Kindersley)

Books (Fiction)   *Dolphins at Daybreak.* Mary Pope Osborne (Random House)
Falling for a Dolphin. Heathcote Williams (Jonathan Cape)

Videos (Nonfiction)   *Dolphins.* (Image Entertainment)
Dolphins: The Wild Side. (National Geographic)
Dolphins with Robin Williams. (PBS Home Video)

Videos (Fiction)   *Flipper.* (MGM)

BOTTLENOSE DOLPHIN QUICK FACTS

Average weight of adults
330 to 1,435 pounds (150 to 650 kilograms)

Average length of adults
6 to 12 feet (1.8 to 3.7 meters) long.

Number of teeth
76 to 100, which range in length from 1 to 3 inches (2.5 to 7.6 centimeters)

Length of life
Females: up to 35 years
Males: up to 25 years

Special feature
Colors can range from very light to very dark gray on the back and creamy
white to light gray on the belly. Some bottlenose dolphins even have spots or
stripes on their bellies! Scientists think this is due to mating between bottlenoses
and other species of dolphins.

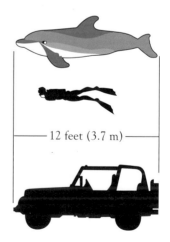

12 feet (3.7 m)

WEB SITES

If you have your own computer and Internet access, great! If not, most libraries have Internet access. The Internet changes every day, and web sites come and go. We believe the following sites are likely to last and give the best, most appropriate links for readers to find out more about the oceans, whales, and other sea life.

To get started, enter the word "museums" in a general search engine. See if you can find a museum web page that has exhibits on ocean mammals and oceanography. If any of these museums are close to home, you can visit them in person!

www.yahooligans.com
This is a huge search engine and a great research tool for anything you might want to know. For information on whales, click on Animals under the Science & Nature heading. From the Animals page, you can hear or see whales and dolphins by clicking on Animal Sounds or Animal Pictures.

Or you may want to plug some words into the search engine to see what Yahooligans can find for you. Some words related to Bottlenose Dolphins are *captive dolphins*, *echolocation*, *cetaceans*, and *transient dolphins*.

kids.discovery.com/guides/animals/ under_water.html
Don't miss the topics Whale Attack, Animal Emotions, and The Ultimate Guide: Dolphins. You'll read the latest information, see up-close photos, and take amazing underwater tours.

kids.discovery.com/KIDS/thelist.html
This section of *Kids Discovery* offers real-life adventure. Click on THE List and check out numbers 27, 39, and 61.

www.enchantedlearning.com/
Go to Zoom School and click on Whale Activities and Whale Dictionary for games, information sheets, and great links for many species of whales, including orcas, bottlenose dolphins, blue whales, sperm whales, right whales, humpback whales, and others.

www.whaleclub.com
The *Whale Club* is a great place to go to talk to other whale fans, talk to whale experts, and find out the latest news about all the whales in the world.

whale.wheelock.edu
The *WhaleNet* is packed full of the latest whale research information. Some is way cool! Click on the Students and then the WhaleNet Index button to find more buttons and links that will help you find whale videos, hear echolocation, or ask a whale expert a question.

GLOSSARY

You can find these words on the pages listed. Reading a word in a sentence helps you understand it even better.

adaptation (ad-ap-TAY-shun) — a change made that makes survival easier in a certain place or around certain other living things 8

adapted (uh-DAPT-ed) — changed to better fit a living thing to survival in a certain environment 8, 10

alien (AY-lee-uhn) — strange 6, 20

behavior (bih-HAYV-yuhr) — the way animals act 8

calf (KAF) — a bottlenose dolphin less than two years old; plural: **calves** (KAVZ) 14, 18

communicate (kuh-MYOO-nuh-KAYT) — to share information or comfort 14

echolocation (EK-oh-loh-KAY-shun) — the process of sending and receiving sound to learn about an object or an animal 16

habitat (HAB-uh-tat) — a place where a person or animal lives 12

melon (MEL-uhn) — a mass of fatty tissue in a bottlenose dolphin's forehead which, scientists believe, dolphins use for making sounds and for echolocation 16

orcas (OR-kahz) — also known as "killer whales" but in fact the largest kind of dolphin 16

prey (PRAY) — animals that are hunted for food 10, 12

signature whistle (SIG-nuh-chur WISS-uhl) — the noise a bottlenose dolphin makes that is either its own "name" or the "name" of another dolphin 14

INDEX

24